# WRITE YOUR LIFE RIGHT

## JOURNALING YOUR WAY TO SUCCESS

TAMARA BOYNTON HOWARD, MPH

# PREFACE

Friday the 13th, was one of the best and worst days of my life. I was fired. My ego immediately went to, "How dare they fire me?" By the time I cleaned out my office, I landed on, "Thank God they fired me." A few days later, "What the hell am I going to do now?" I didn't have a backup plan because this *was* my back up plan. I had furloughed attending a doctoral graduate program because I was not sure what I actually wanted to do with my life. Education seemed like a safe bet so I became a teacher and eventually transitioned to other education-related jobs.

I started working at this job on a part-time basis while in my master's program and was promoted three times over the course of the first year. It was a cool gig and thought I might just retire from there. The only problem was there was no room for growth and I made less than most housekeepers at neighboring schools. I was already at the top position that I could entertain in my department. To get a new position would only be a lateral move into another department. The amount of stress I encountered on a daily basis was ri-dic-u-lous! Every part of my life suffered, but I loved working with college students.

The people I was responsible for helping brought me so much joy that I tried to overlook everything else. (Can you relate?) When management of our department changed, I tried to be as open and transparent with the new person in charge. I asked for help when I needed it. I went above and beyond the call of duty. I built relationships with similar organizations in the community and connected people with resources never before available. However, I also refused to do unethical stuff. I had morals and values that I followed without compromise. In the end, I realized I misjudged the office politics at play.

The day I had a full on melt down because I was called back early from my lunch break to be chastised about labels is probably the day I should have quit but I stayed. I didn't have a backup plan and I still had a year to go in my master's program. I remember walking to my office repeatedly - saying with a deep passion mixed with anger, "I wish they would just fire me so I can get unemployment!" My coworkers and I all agreed to stay through the end of the summer but to start looking for jobs. Within 2 weeks of my supervisors departure, I was fired.

Luckily, the reasons they used to fire me were never addressed in employee evaluations, reprimanded for or coached on. We did not even have an employee handbook. Standard operating procedures. What are those? In fact, my evaluations were superb. However, they said I was not a team player and that I was insubordinate. It was the biggest lie and blessing of my life.

The first week after I got fired, I simply acted like I was on vacation while continuing my job search. It was a crazy phenomenon. I woke up and it felt like all of my stress had vanished into thin air. I actually noticed that the leaves were beginning to change color. I had fun and went places that I would/could not go before because of my job. The second week after I got fired, I applied for unemployment benefits. The unemployment office had no problem granting my benefits and I got paid for unused vacation and personal time. It wasn't the amount I was used to making, but I would be okay for a little while. It was at this point where I took time to decide what I wanted to do next. I kept applying for jobs as required by the state and I also started to think about what I wanted in the next position.

During one of my trips to the local bookstore, my girlfriend and I made a list of all the things we liked and disliked. You know what? Nothing from any of my previous jobs was on that list. NOTHING! The question became, "Should I stay in the same job market or should I do something different." The pros and cons list for employment seemed pretty clear. It was time to do something different, and freelance writing had my name written all over it.

Step by step, I felt like my entire plan just come together. A former colleague gifted me money. With those funds, I bought a self-help guide to getting published. I saw a one woman show that I liked. I pitched an article to a reputable magazine. Within a few weeks, I got a call asking for the article and a contract in the mail. It was an amazing feeling! I felt like I was finally doing something that I was supposed to be doing. It felt genuine, authentic, easy, and so –well– me!

This period of my life was the beginning of Write Your Life Right (WYLR). The lists, the processing, the trying to figure out where my life went off track all started at this point. It actually took me a couple of years to nail down the specifics. I didn't know any other way but the traditional journaling method of document-ing my thoughts. During this time, I began to meditate on a regu-lar basis; I started devouring spiritually based books, movies, and television programs. Some of what was said made sense, but other components just didn't fit with my beliefs.

Upon connecting with a meditation book, I started journaling differently. My intention was to replace the sitting meditation with writing. This writing was different from what I was used to. It was intense and uncensored. The writing kept leading to more questions about me, my beliefs, my purpose, and my desires. I kept hearing, "Why do you think that?" and "What are you going to do differently?" And I kept writing. The answers unfolded with ease and grace. When I look back at those journals, it is easy to see the barriers that I had constructed but it easier to see how each one was systematically torn down.

I recognized this process when I was transitioning from a horrible job. However, I realized I had used this same technique throughout my school life to reach academic goals, in my personal life to nurture my self-esteem and self worth, and my romantic life to finally acknowledge the love of my life. I hope you gain as much or more from this process.

# 1: THE RIGHT BELIEFS

Journaling taught me there was a reason my bank account *felt* like it was permanently set on low. In a nutshell: my beliefs. The story I had been telling myself was that I needed a better job, another degree, a better college, better networks, a mentor, and come from the right family. I didn't have the right credentials to make the right connections with the right people. There was nothing right about my life, thus I did not deserve more than I already had.

The crazy thing about these beliefs, were they were not visible to the naked eye. To the outside world, I was happy, supportive, workaholic, and in love with my then girlfriend/now wife. However, I felt like I had been hoodwinked and bamboozled into believing the American dream was real. Working hard, getting good grades, staying out of trouble had only gotten me at best middle management type jobs and a whole bunch of debt. I had poor communication skills because I didn't know what I wanted let alone how to articulate them with so many feelings of unworthiness.

While writing my life right, I openly admitted I had not been pursuing my passion and when I was, it had nothing to do with my creative spark, intuition, or even my truest desires. Competing and comparing me to other people's accomplishments had been keeping me miserable and stuck in someone else's version of my life. I didn't want most of the things people were bragging about so life felt much lighter when I could admit that to myself. I could admit that I was happy with some things in my life that other people put down.

Nothing can stop you from attaining what you want. No credit score or criminal background check has the capacity to keep you from living your dream. Ask any rapper that has gone to jail. Ask any person who has ever filed bankruptcy. Ask any overweight actor. Ask any ugly model. Ask any illiterate writer. If they can live their dream—you can surely live yours. They aren't better than you and no one deserves success or to live the fairy tale life any more than you do. We all have the capacity to live the life we want and through the journaling exercises in this book, you will finally identify those wants and start living your life to acquire them.

Chapter 1 Takeaways:
- We are good enough to receive all of our heart's desires.
- Be honest about your desires.

# 2: THE RIGHT WRITE TOOLS

In order to write your life right, you must have paper and a writing utensil. You might be tempted to pick up any paper you have lying around the house. If that is all you have, then certainly start where you can. In my perfect world, you would have access to a bound journal. A journal with a perfect bound will keep all of your papers together. It will be easier for you to return to your idea and continue writing. Loose sheets of paper or legal pads can easily be torn or ripped from the notebook which also means they can be easily lost. In building ritual, I also suggest that you have a dedicated writing utensil. If you aren't anxious about finding your writing tools, your process will

Growing up, I was obsessed with having a diary. The first one I can remember had a heart shaped lock with a skeleton key. With that heart and key, my ideas were sacred, precious, and protected. I hid my diary in several places: sometimes under my mattress, at other times in my closet, and last but not least under my pillow. It never seemed like it was enough though. I was always afraid that someone would find my diary and read my deepest secret: who I had a crush on! My world was shattered every time I moved and realized my diary was "lost" –never to be seen again.

That didn't keep me from wanting to write. I consistently begged and pleaded for more notebooks and diaries. When the electronic diaries hit the market, I was enamored. What little girl of my persuasion wouldn't be? The electronic diaries were so cute! Usually, it was a shade of pink or purple and featured the girly pop icon of the day: Barbie, Jem, or someone similar. I loved the idea of password protecting my diary. I could leave it anywhere and not worry that someone would guess my password. It was the perfect solution until the battery went dead. In my family, if it wasn't a triple A, double A, or 9 volt battery, it didn't get replaced! Can you relate?

You might think that this made me more vigilant about protecting my thoughts, poems, prayers, and goals written in these sacred moments. But time after time, each diary disappeared. They could be in landfills or someone's home. I have no clue. I have no record of any ideas or thoughts from the time I received my first diary until I started writing my life right. Those ideas belong to the universe and are simply out there somewhere.

I sometimes worry that they will resurface at an inopportune time, but then I realized they are just a reflection of me at a particular moment in time. I probably cursed, had damning confessions, and was vulnerable, scared, and maybe even brutally honest. I could have misunderstood a situation, but in the end they were my ideas. They could be true and not true all in the same instance. Even still, ensure that you have tools that allow you to protect your writings and keep them together safely.

Chapter 2 Takeaways:
- Treat yourself to a bound journal to keep your ideas together and safe.
- Designate a writing utensil or computer.

# 3: SAFETY CONSIDERA-TIONS

As I have embarked on this adventure, I encountered people for whom writing was not safe. Writing their thoughts and dreams put them in danger, caused pain, and heartache. At the first Write Your Life Right workshop, no one mentioned safety as a concern. People blissfully wrote for three hours about their hearts intentions. At the second Write Your Life Right workshop, I was confronted with multiple women who were afraid to write their own thoughts for themselves. There was no sharing required. There was no "danger" as far as I could tell. Yet, there was a block, hindering expression for a few people in the group. I was at a complete loss. I didn't know what to do. So I just listened to them.

I heard my clients. They discussed times where they didn't feel safe writing, where there words were used against them, where their writings actually put them in danger. Abusive relationships whether from a parent, spouse, loved ones, and even court systems exist. I do not pretend that they don't. To write your life right, a sense of safety and trust must exist. Thus, over time, I have created a few safety recommendations.

**Sharing:** Write Your Life Right entries should not be shared with others. Besides being an energy drainer, discussed in Chapter 4, you do not know the intentions or motives of any other person. You could assume or guess based on your previous interactions with them, but the truth of the matter is you do not know. One client shared how her ex-husband used her previous writings against her in their divorce settlement. He threatened to tell the judge some things she admitted to doing in her writing in order to broker more visitation time with their kids. Another client would share what she wrote but then not accomplish anything on the list. She mistook her sharing as doing something and that simply was not what WYLR was meant to be. Keeping your work private is one of the keys to Write Your Life Right.

**Safe space:** Writing can get intense- really quickly. While some people like writing in cafes or coffee house, others will enjoy their kitchen table, bed, or a park. When determining your space, ask yourself the following: If I burst into tears would I be okay here? Can I go to the bathroom and come back with my items undisturbed? Will I be concerned if someone read this over my shoulder? Unfortunately, your home might not be a safe space. Do you have a friend that would want to travel on this journey with you? Could you write in your car? Where will you write?

**Safe storage:** Who has access to the space will help you de-termine where your journal will be stored: on a bookshelf, under your pillow, or under your mattress? I keep my journal in a drawer so that if I have visitors, a random person won't be reading my thoughts. One of my clients has a "God Box". It is a combination lock box that can be decorated using traditional scrapbooking sup-plies. The lock box could be stored under a bed, closet, cabinet, or drawer. Using a combination instead of a key adds additional safe-ty measures so that the worry of losing the key is eliminated. Where will you keep your journal?

**Computer-based journaling:** If you do not have a lot of pri-vacy, you may prefer to utilize online sources. First, create a new password protected user account on your computer. This should not be the same account that you use for everything else. This may be enough. Just make sure the documents you create in this account are not accessible in other accounts on the same computer.

If you need or like the ability of your documents being accessible to you on the go, consider using a cloud or blogging resource. These applications are usually free and password protected adding another layer of privacy. Some sites even allow you to password protect individual posts. How awesome is that?

If you need even more security, a privacy filter can be fit to your computer screen. The screen blocks the readability of your computer from persons on either side of you. Please note a privacy screen does not block the visibility of someone who is directly behind you. You may have to get creative and use a combination of these suggestions.

Chapter 3 Takeaways:
• Protect your physical and emotional space.
• There are tools you can use to make your writing journey more private.

# 4: THE RIGHT SUPPORT

"Create a support system that nourishes your dream." Your support system should include positive and supportive people. They see the best in and for you. This supportive tribe already knows that anything is possible. Essentially, these creative thinkers help you to see that your dreams can be bigger, better, and impact you in a more profound way. In words and actions, they encourage you because in the face of someone else's destructive opinion, you must push forward. A great support system will help you do that in a constructive way.

Mind you, there may not be a lot of people in your support system. It may be as small as one or two people. It could be more. Have you ever heard the saying, "Do not share your problems with other people; 20% don't care and 80% are glad you have them." Let me tweak that statement: "Do not share your ideas with other people; 95% don't believe in you or are jealous they didn't have the idea first, and 5% are genuinely happy for you and will help you reach your dreams." I call the 95%: naysayers and the 5% are your amen corner. How do you know the difference between a "naysayer" and a member of your "Amen Corner"?

## NAYSAYERS

Naysayers are the primary reason you need a strong support system. Naysayers display the following characteristics:
- complain all of the time;
- gossip;
- have a negative outlook on life;
- their problems are always someone else's fault;

- they are secretly (or not so secretly) jealous of you and gossip about you behind your back;
- they question your motives for dreaming and/or your reasons for attending school or getting more training;
- they may even describe you as a sell-out, a wishful thinker, unrealistic, or tell you that you live in a fantasy world.

Don't fret. If you happen upon a person you *thought* was in your amen corner but they are actually a naysayer—it is okay. You will need to put some distance between your dream and that person. Do not share anymore of your ideas with the naysayer. If asked about it, just say something simple, "Thanks for asking. It's a work in progress." Then, change the subject.

If you are the naysayer, you don't have to continue to be a naysayer. The first step is to work on yourself so you can believe in yourself. Therapy works. Check out my website for resources. Next, identify your dreams, get a support system and get to work on them. I know that you want to be successful. You have this book. You simply do not have enough experience with success to stop the constant criticism.

# AMEN CORNER

If your goal is to care about or believe in someone else more than yourself, then fine. Keep surrounding yourself with people who do not have the propensity to support you in attaining your dreams.

I am in no way saying to leave your husband, wife, or life partner. But to really move yourself forward, you will need to have a support system that can fill that void in your life. It does not have to be a spouse, mom, dad, or even a relative. It could be your therapist or a co-worker. You never know, you may find this person at school, work, online or even a networking event.

Eventually, you will need to be able to answer clearly: "Why do you want this dream?" Or better yet: "Why have you been putting off going for it?" Separating yourself from naysayers and connecting with your "Amen Corner" will help you in this process.

I call this group your "amen corner" because they have your back no matter what. I tend to think that these people are divinely placed in your life for the purpose of helping you get to your next level. They try to help you figure out how things can work instead of always telling you why they can't or won't work. You do not always have to look for these people. Sometimes, they seek you out or they will just show up! They will mentor you and show you the ropes.

Let me be clear, your amen corner will challenge you to be your best self. They will not accept mediocrity and they will not accept you being flaky with your dreams. They will not always say yes or cosign foolishness. Got it? Your amen corner is a supporter who helps you stay accountable to your dreams.

Chapter 4 Takeaways:
- Connect with people who support your drive.
- Run like hell away from naysayers.

# 5: THE WYLR PROCESS

The only way you can do Write Your Life Right wrong is to not do it. Whenever I do a Write Your Life Right (WYLR) workshop, I usually get one of three responses: enthusiasm, trepidation, or outright defiance. It usually sounds like this: "I'm not a good writer/speller/etc." "I don't know what I want." "I can't write." "My mind doesn't work like that." "I have a learning disability." I hear you. In school, writing was the bane of my existence. Although I enjoyed writing, my teachers used to nit-pick every little error. "Don't write on the last line of the paper." "Did you plagiarize?" "Proofread. Proofread. Proofread!" Uggh! So annoying!

This is not the space for that. There are no grammar rules in Write Your Life Right. I have no desire to nag you into perfection. Writing does not always require words; it is simply putting pen to paper. It can show up as doodle, drawing, coloring, poetry, expressive writing, intuitive writing, or any variation thereof. People ask, "Then, why do I have to write it down?" Consider this: what important thing do you not write down?

I cannot think of one significant thing that is not written down. Darnita Howard, a designer and workshop participant said, "It's amazing how we bind ourselves to others through contracts but we do not do the same with our own desires."

From birthdays, marriages, and anniversaries, to a job description or who you want to be President of the United States; every important thing is documented. Write it down, sign it and date it. Are your dreams and goals important? Is your happiness important? Do you have an idea of success that does not fit with your family's and friends' definitions? <u>Then, it is imperative that you set the agenda for your life, clarify your desires while journaling through the barriers, and align your actions with those desires.</u>

Contrary to popular belief, your success is not solely dependent upon your resume, cover letter, or social media account. The number of likes on your status, followers of your blog, or retweets of your status update has no bearing on whether or not you will thrive. Your triumph depends on three things: your desire, your commitment, and your perceived self-worth. When these three constructs are aligned, success in whatever you want can be realized.

### STEP 1 - WRITE IT DOWN, MAKE IT PLAIN

With journaling, you begin to set the agenda for your life. The ultimate clarity is needed during this process. You don't want to write just for the sake of writing. It is akin to creating a contract with _yourself_. It is an act of faith, a commitment, and confirmation that this thing, relationship, or experience that you want can and will happen. Your desires are the agenda. Your actions quicken the process and your perceived self-worth directly influences the rate of manifestation.

Have you ever been to a meeting that did not have an agenda? I have and those meetings are usually a pain in the arse. They are the biggest waste of time, space, and energy. A life without an agenda is equivalent to that boring meeting: an energy drainer. It literally sucks the sparkle right out of you.

So what's on your agenda? Most successful people and even companies have an agenda. Yes, agendas have gotten a bad reputation over the years as people have become collateral damage. Even in this moment, I have a little angst. An agenda can feel like someone is trying to manipulate something in ones favor. However, in this context, let's look at journaling and agenda setting as the *reveal of unconscious thoughts*. It does not require you to influence anyone. It is the impetus for your awe inspiring life. In fact, if you do not have your own agenda, you usually end completing tasks on someone else's list. Don't be that person for long. Start the process, stick with it, and watch your wildest dreams become fulfilled.

Once you start to acknowledge your wants...dig into the underlying feelings you want to experience that are associated with those wants. For example, if you feel like you deserve a better job, bigger house, or better car—go for it! That's right, the bigger the dream, the better life can be but don't stop at the dream.

In your journal, ask yourself these questions?
• What do I want?
• Why do I want it?

## STEP 2: COMMIT

One of my friends used to say, "In order to have success, one must do something." I completely agree. Luckily, journaling is doing something. The secret to this is that the ideas may be stored on the page, but they do not live there. Once you figure out what you really want, you have to commit to it. Use the journaling to help you eliminate the barriers then bring your actions into alignment with your desires.

You have to want this so much that you do not contradict those wants with your actions. For instance, if you want to lose weight then you know that eating a carton of ice cream everyday may not help you reach your goal. If you do make the choice to eat the whole carton, is weight loss your actual goal or is it something else? Do you want to be able to buy nicer clothes at affordable prices? Do you want a lover who admires your curves with no complaints? Here is an opportunity to quiet the voices of all of those people you have listened to over the years.

Get quiet. Be honest with yourself about your heart's truest desires. Have huge dreams and do not shy away from them. Then, listen!

In your journal, ask yourself these questions?
- What is it I really want?
- What lies am I believing about myself that keep me from reaching my goals?
- How do I eliminate the barriers to my dreams?

## STEP 3: BELIEVE
I have met with a lot of people who have a dream but they aren't going for it. For whatever reason, they don't think that their dream is "realistic". I suspect that people don't go for their dreams for a few reasons:
- They don't know what they want.
- Someone told them their dream was unattainable.
- They don't believe they are good enough – or deserving of their dream.
- They have so many dreams they don't know what to do first or where to start.
- [Insert any other excuse here!]

I get it. I've been there and done that. I made a decision to go for it anyway! This is the key. You have to go for your dreams anyway. It doesn't matter what other people say, you have to believe in your dreams. You have to know that the work you put into your journal is allowing you to tap into your intuition. It all starts with writing. What would make you happy? A million dollars? A passionate romantic love affair? A person to sit on the porch with you when you get old? A nap? A piece of chocolate?

This process works every time. Even if you say, "Tamara, I write stuff down all the time but it doesn't always work." My response will always be, "Did you really want it? Did you have a great support system? When you wrote it down, did you believe it would happen? Did it happen but not in the way in which you expected it?" My guess is that these questions hold the solution to your breakthrough.

Whatever you believe you deserve will bear fruit in your life. I write what I want and before I know it, I can check it off when I get it. In as much, it is time for you to do the same. Dream big, get a support system, and write it down! Any desire you want can be fulfilled. Go for it! Your dreams are waiting!

Whatever you want, you can have. I have used this process for nearly every area in my life: love relationships, friendships, apartment search, wedding, business, vacations, decorating my space, school assignments – and even basic life decisions. In whatever part of my life where I want to experience success or just something new, I run it through the Write Your Life Right process.

Chapter 5 Takeaways:
• Set the agenda.
• Sign and date each entry.
• Journal to gain clarity and remove barriers.

- Believe in your dreams and bring your actions into alignment with those dreams.

# 6: YOU CAN DO THIS!

Just in case it has not been made abundantly clear: You cannot live someone else's dream. Well, you can, but you might not be that happy about it. If your mom thinks you should be a doctor but you really want to be a dancer, which dream should get the most attention? What if you want to live abroad but your parents refuse to sign the financial aid paperwork?

The dream doesn't really matter, it's how you want to feel that matters. Would you be upset if your dream was to be a parent, and that showed up as you being selected to be a god-parent or adoptive parent? Some people would be really upset while others would be ecstatic and feel blessed.

Don't hold so tight to the dream itself and remember how you want to feel. It's easy to get caught up in the details. However, the imagination is limitless. The boundaries exist because we put them there. As your life changes, remember to be grateful at every stage. If it gets too hard, remember to go to your amen corner and don't take your frustrations out on other people.

Chapter 6 Takeaways:
- Allow breathing room in your dream.
- Show gratitude and tap into your support system.

# 7: JOURNAL PROMPTS

Here are some journaling prompts to get you started. You can go in any order. You can use these or you can choose to answer a question of your own choosing.

1. What do you want?
2. Why do you want it?
3. Why haven't you received it already?
4. Where did that belief come from?
5. Who do you need to forgive?
6. What about your belief is false?
7. What about your belief Is true?
8. What do you need to know?
9. What would you tell your favorite person about this situation?
10. What are you waiting for?

Stop reading and get busy!
Seriously!
P.S.Remember, It's not easy, but it is attainable.

ARE YOU READY TO CHANGE YOUR LIFE?
ORDER NOW
WRITE YOUR LIFE RIGHT
A Guided Journal
TAMARA BOYNTON HOWARD, MPH
LINK IN BIO
The Write Your Life Right workbook is a guided journaling experience to explore your thoughts and feelings, figure out what's holding you back, and create a plan for the future.

www.ingramcontent.com/pod-product-compliance
Lightning Source LLC
Chambersburg PA
CBHW071811020426
42331CB00008B/2459